SORTING PLANTS

What is a Flower?

by Sally Hewitt

WESTERN ISLES LIBRARIES	
30776067J	
Bertrams	03.08.07
J580	£4.99

Aladdin/Watts
London • Sydney

D0248740

You are **alive**.

A **plant** is **alive** too.

Like you, a plant **grows**.

4

34134 00061598 6

Leabharlainn nan Eilean Siar

WITHDRAWN

Note to Parents and Teachers

The READING ABOUT: STARTERS series introduces key science vocabulary to young children while encouraging them to discover and understand the world around them. The series works as a set of graded readers in three levels.

LEVEL 1: BEGINNING TO READ follows guidelines set out in the National Curriculum for Year 1 in schools. These books can be read alone or as part of guided or group reading. Each book has three sections:

• Information pages that introduce new words. These key words appear in bold throughout the book for easy recognition.
• A lively story that recalls this vocabulary and encourages children to use these words when they talk and write.
• A quiz and word search ask children to look back and recall what they have read.

WHAT IS A FLOWER? looks at SORTING PLANTS. Below are some activities related to the questions on the information spreads that parents, carers and teachers can use to discuss and develop further ideas and concepts:

p. 5 *What do you need to help you grow?* You could also ask children to think about other differences between animals and plants.

p. 7 *What do you think happens to a plant without water?* Ask the children if they can think of a fair test in which some plants are watered and others are not.

p. 9 *A plant left in the dark doesn't grow well. Why?* You could also explore other reasons why a plant may not grow well, e.g. pests and disease, pots too small.

p. 11 *Why do you think some leaves are prickly?* Ask children to think of animals that eat plants, from caterpillar to giraffe. Show them plants that have been munched!

p. 17 *Can you find seeds inside the fruit you eat?* Ask children to compare seed sizes from apple pips and melon seeds to stones in peaches. Contrast with tiny pips on the outside of strawberries.

p. 19 *Why do you think the root grows first?* Could also ask children to suggest why it is important not to pull up growing plants.

p. 21 *Have you seen plants growing in strange places?* You could take children for a walk in your local area and challenge them to find plants growing in as many places as possible.

p. 23 *What fruit and vegetables do you like to eat?* Ask children to guess what various vegetables are, e.g. parsnips – roots. Could discuss why plants develop tasty fruits/berries.

J580
307760675

SCHOOL
LIBRARY
STOCK

Co-ordinator,
Twickenham

er Senior
ion, Westminster
University

Series Consultants
Anne Fussell – Early Years Teacher and University Tutor, Westminster College, Oxford Brookes University

David Fussell – C.Chem., FRSC

WITHDRAWN

CONTENTS

PAPERBACK EDITION PRINTED 2007
© Aladdin Books Ltd 2004

Designed and produced by
Aladdin Books Ltd
2/3 Fitzroy Mews
London W1T 6DF

First published in 2004
in Great Britain by
Franklin Watts
338 Euston Road
London NW1 3BH

Franklin Watts Australia
Hachette Children's Books
Level 17/207 Kent Street
Sydney NSW 2000

A catalogue record for this
book is available from the
British Library.
Dewey Classification: 580
ISBN 978 07496 7519 6

Printed in Malaysia

All rights reserved

Editor: Jim Pipe

Design: Flick, Book Design
and Graphics

Thanks to: The pupils of Trafalgar
Infants School, Twickenham • Lynne
Thompson • The pupils and teachers
of Trafalgar Junior School,
Twickenham, and St. Nicholas C.E.
Infant School, Wallingford.

Photocredits:
*l-left, r-right, b-bottom, t-top,
c-centre, m-middle*
All photos supplied by PBD except
for: Front cover tm, tr, 3b, 10r,
11br, 13tr, 14, 15tl, 15tr, 15bl,
17b, 31ml, 32mrc — Flick Smith.
2tl, 9b, 12, 13b, 19 all, 32mlc —
Jim Pipe. 2ml, 16t — Bruce
Fritz/USDA. 3ml, 15br — Peggy
Greb/USDA. 4, 8b, 32tl — Ken
Hammond/USDA. 5tr, 20t —
Corel. 5b, 21tl — Photodisc. 6,
27tl, 27bl, 29tl, 32tr — Select
Pictures. 8tl, 9tr, 10tl, 20ml,
21br, 32bl, 32mrt — Corbis. 11t
— Brand X Pictures. 17tr —
Patrick Tregenza/USDA. 22t, 23
all, 31tr, 31bl, 32mlt, 32br —
Stockbyte.

A big tree is a **plant**.
It **grows** much bigger
than you!

A tiny daisy is a **plant**
too. It is much smaller
than you.

• What do you need to help you grow?

All plants have stems,
leaves, and **roots**.
Some plants have flowers too.

Plants need **water** to grow.

Roots suck up **water** from the soil.

Water goes up the stem
and into the leaves and flowers.

• What do you think happens to a plant without water?

Animals have to hunt
and search for **food**.
We can buy our **food** in stores.

8

Plants don't have to hunt for **food**
or buy **food** in stores.
Plants make their **food** from **sunlight!**

• A plant left in the dark doesn't grow well. Why?

My new word: **leaves**

Leaves are all kinds of
different shapes.
Tulip **leaves** are long and pointed.
Holly **leaves** are shiny and prickly.

Some trees have **leaves** that change color and drop in fall.

Other trees keep their green **leaves** all year round.

• Why do you think some leaves are prickly?

The **stem** supports the plant.
A tree has a strong, woody **stem**
called a **trunk** to hold it upright.

Water plants have **stems** that wave in the water.

Climbing plants have **stems** that bend and curl.

• Which parts of your body can you bend and curl?

Many **flowers** have colorful **petals** and a sweet smell.
Insects see and smell the **flowers** and come looking for food.

A bluebell is the shape of a bell.
A buttercup is the color of butter.
A rose has a sweet smell.

Bluebell   **Buttercup**

Pansy   **Rose**

• Find flowers with different colors and shapes.
Look for flowers with patterns too, like a pansy.   15

The flower is the part
of the plant where
seeds are made.

A **seed** grows into a new plant.

16

A peach **seed** is a hard **pit**.

Dandelion **seeds** fly away on fluffy parachutes.

• Can you find seeds inside the fruit you eat?

My new words: **seedling, shoot**

Baby plants are called
seedlings.
You can plant a bean and
watch a **seedling** grow.

18

First the root grows down.

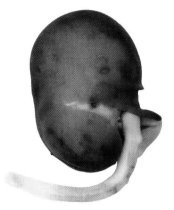

Then the **shoot**
grows up.

Green leaves open
out. The stem grows
thick and strong.

• Why do you think the root grows first?

Plants grow everywhere.

They grow in the **park**, in the **garden**, on walls, and on paths.

20

Cactus plants grow in hot, dry **deserts**.

They don't need much water.

Tiny flowers grow near cold **mountain** tops.

• Have you seen plants growing in strange places?

Animals and people eat plants. Cows munch **grass**. **Fruit** and **vegetables** help to keep you strong and healthy.

We eat every part of a plant.

Carrots are roots.

Celery sticks are stems.

Broccoli is lots of tiny flowers.

Celery

Carrots

Broccoli

• What fruit and vegetables do you like to eat?

Now read the story of **The Mystery Egg**.
Watch for words about **plants**.

"I've got something for you two," says Grami. She opens her hand.

"Tiny stripy eggs!" says Tom.
"Tiny stripy **seeds**!" says Ally.

24

"Let's see who is right," laughs Grami.

Tom makes a warm nest for his "egg." "It will hatch soon," he says.

Ally **plants** her **seed** in some soil. She **waters** it. She puts it in **sunlight**. "It will **grow** soon," she says.

Tom keeps his "egg" warm. He waits for it to hatch.

Nothing happens! Ally **waters** her **seed**.

Soon, a little **shoot** appears. "Look Tom, it's a **seedling!**" says Ally.

Green **leaves grow** on Ally's **seedling**.

The **stem grows** thick and strong.

Tom helps Ally **plant** her **seedling** in the **garden**.

"Look, there are the **roots**," says Tom.

Ally's **plant grows** taller.

"Look, there's a little bud!" says Ally.

Tom is worried. "My egg will hatch soon!" he says.

Ally **waters** her **plant**.
The sun shines on it.
The little bud opens.
It's a sunflower with
yellow **petals**!

Grami comes to see Tom and Ally.
Ally shows her the sunflower.

Tom looks sad.
"Cheer up,"
says Grami.

"Here are some
more **seeds** for
you to **plant**."
Tom smiles.

Tell the story of how
a **plant grows**. Begin
with **planting** a **seed**.

Can you draw a
picture of a **plant**?
Write a label to show
each part.

Leaves

Stem

Roots

QUIZ

How do **plants** make their **food**?

Answer on page 9

Why do insects visit **flowers**?

Answer on page 14

What happens when you **plant** seeds?

Answer on page 16

What part of a **plant** is a carrot?

Answer on page 23

Did you know the answers? Give yourself a

Do you remember these **plant** words?
Well done! Can you remember any more?

 plant
page 4

roots
page 6

 sunlight
page 9

leaves
page 10

 stem
page 13

flowers
page 15

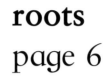

 seeds
page 16

shoot
page 19

 garden
page 20

vegetables
page 23